Maths 4-5
Count to 20

Lynn Huggins-Cooper

Contents

2 Information for parents
4 Clover counts flowers
6 Princess counts to 20
8 Horace has sugar lumps
10 Daffodil counts creatures
12 Fun time!
14 Sebastian dreams of numbers
16 Candy counts in 2s
18 Henrietta counts in 10s
20 Terence looks at numbers
22 Princess gets muddy
24 Fun time!
26 Horace looks and learns

28 Terence counts sacks
30 Candy's cosy bed
32 Gus gets hungry
34 Fun time!
36 Henrietta crunches corn
38 Clover collects leaves
40 Sebastian counts birds
42 Cheeky, Cheery and Chirpy watch a race
44 Daffodil counts dog biscuits
46 Answers
48 Goodbye!

Information for parents

This book makes learning fun. The activities are designed to consolidate the learning experienced by 4–5 year olds as part of the National Curriculum. Do not be concerned if your child is working at a higher or lower level than some of the activities. All children develop at their own pace. You know your child and their capabilities best, so be guided by them. If they find something difficult, come back to it later – they may not be ready.

Do not carry out activities that are beyond them, as they will become frustrated. Once the activities become a chore, you will find it difficult to encourage your child to get involved and engage with the book. Instead, fit the activities into your usual day. When you are carrying out the activities in this book, try to make sure your child has quiet time, free from distractions such as the television. Make sure you are relaxed too and not in a hurry or distracted. Give your child your full attention and they will enjoy the 'together time'. If learning is fun, your child will be eager for more!

Sometimes, if your child is tired or has had a long day, they may not want to carry out activities. Do not become anxious about this; they will carry out the work in their own time. If your child needs extra help or support with an activity, do not worry. Children learn and develop at different rates and your child may need extra time to complete a piece of work.

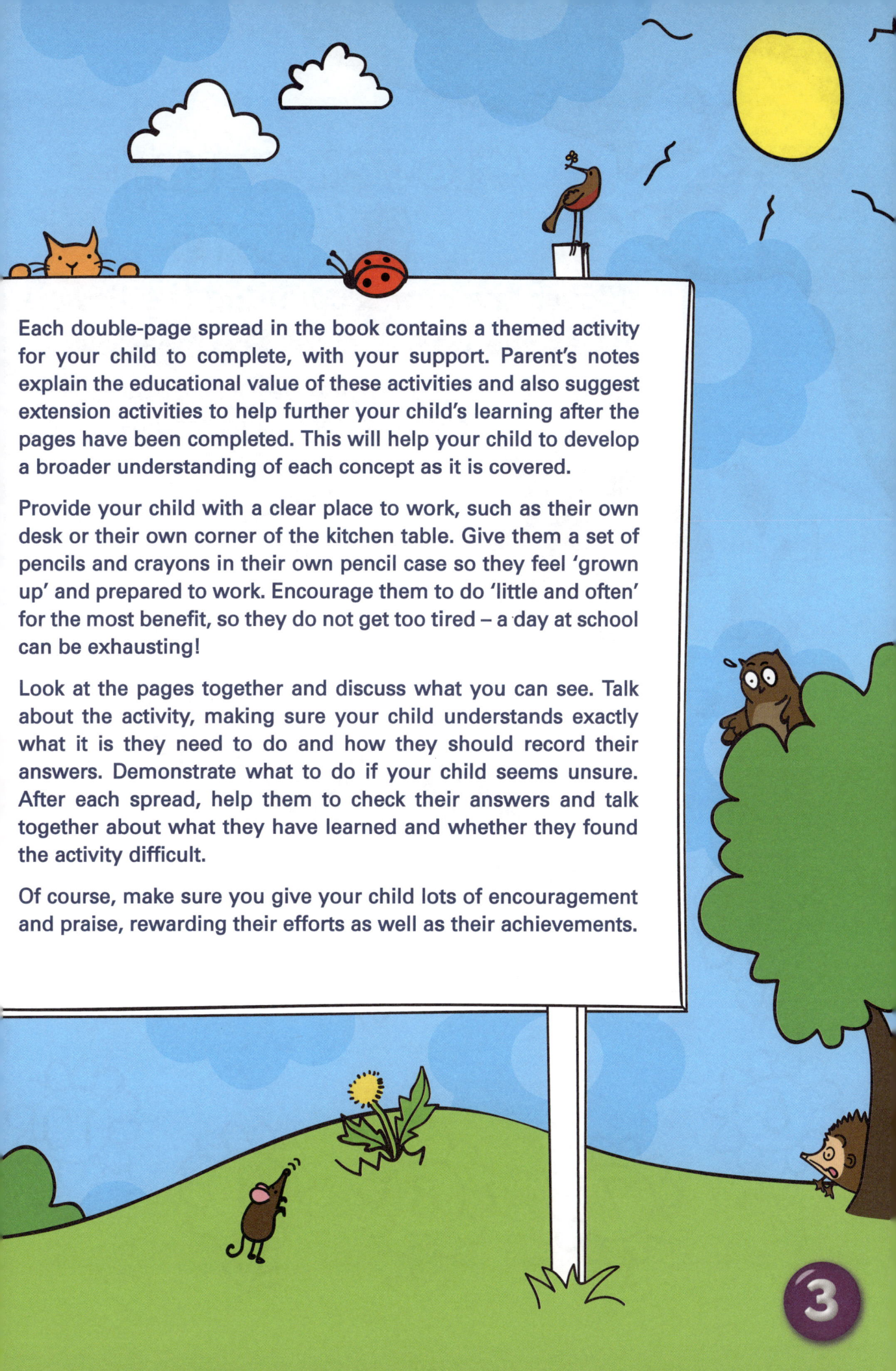

Each double-page spread in the book contains a themed activity for your child to complete, with your support. Parent's notes explain the educational value of these activities and also suggest extension activities to help further your child's learning after the pages have been completed. This will help your child to develop a broader understanding of each concept as it is covered.

Provide your child with a clear place to work, such as their own desk or their own corner of the kitchen table. Give them a set of pencils and crayons in their own pencil case so they feel 'grown up' and prepared to work. Encourage them to do 'little and often' for the most benefit, so they do not get too tired – a day at school can be exhausting!

Look at the pages together and discuss what you can see. Talk about the activity, making sure your child understands exactly what it is they need to do and how they should record their answers. Demonstrate what to do if your child seems unsure. After each spread, help them to check their answers and talk together about what they have learned and whether they found the activity difficult.

Of course, make sure you give your child lots of encouragement and praise, rewarding their efforts as well as their achievements.

Clover counts flowers

Clover the cow is counting the flowers as she walks across the meadow.

Count with her. As you say each number, colour the flower.

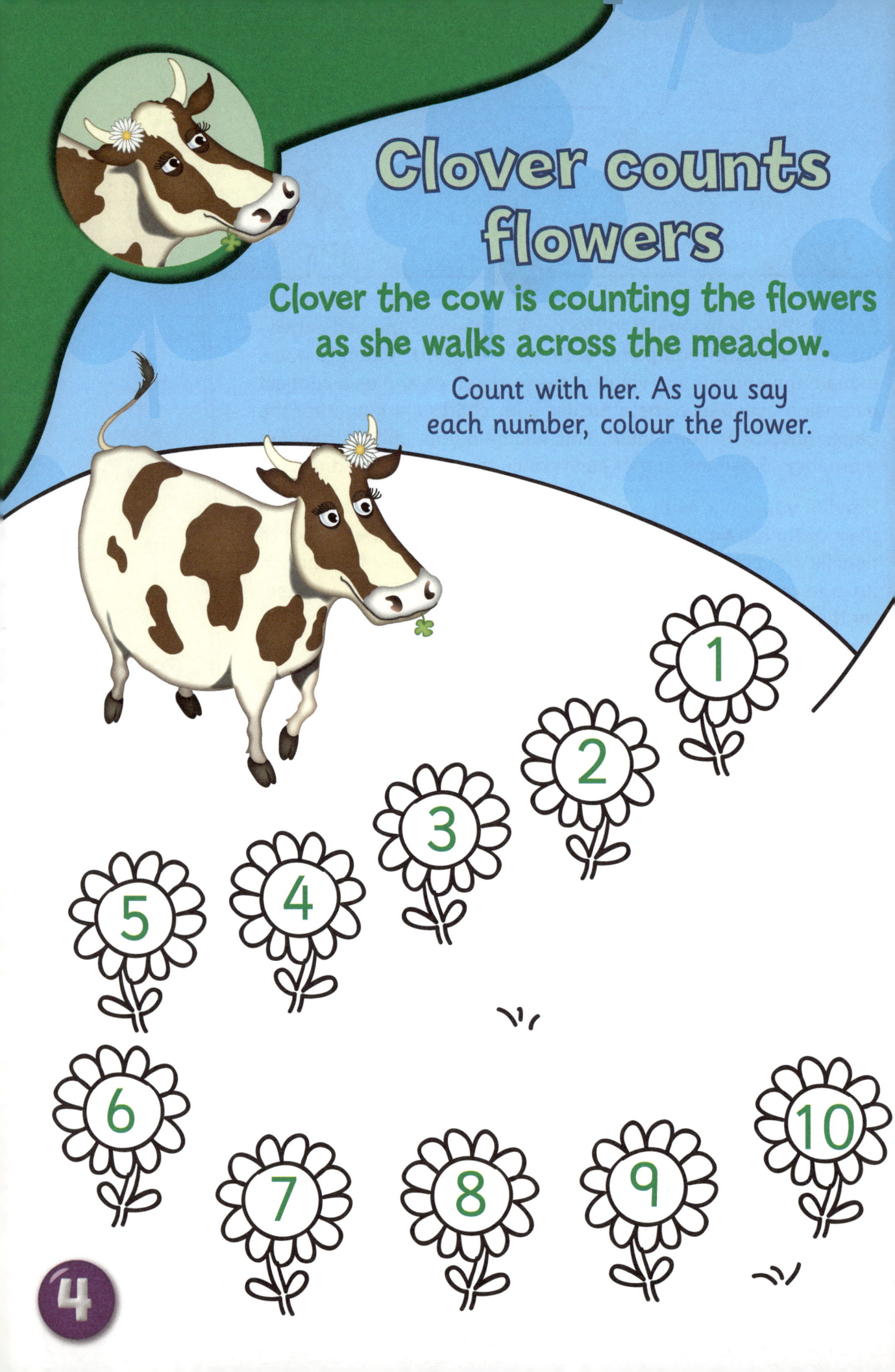

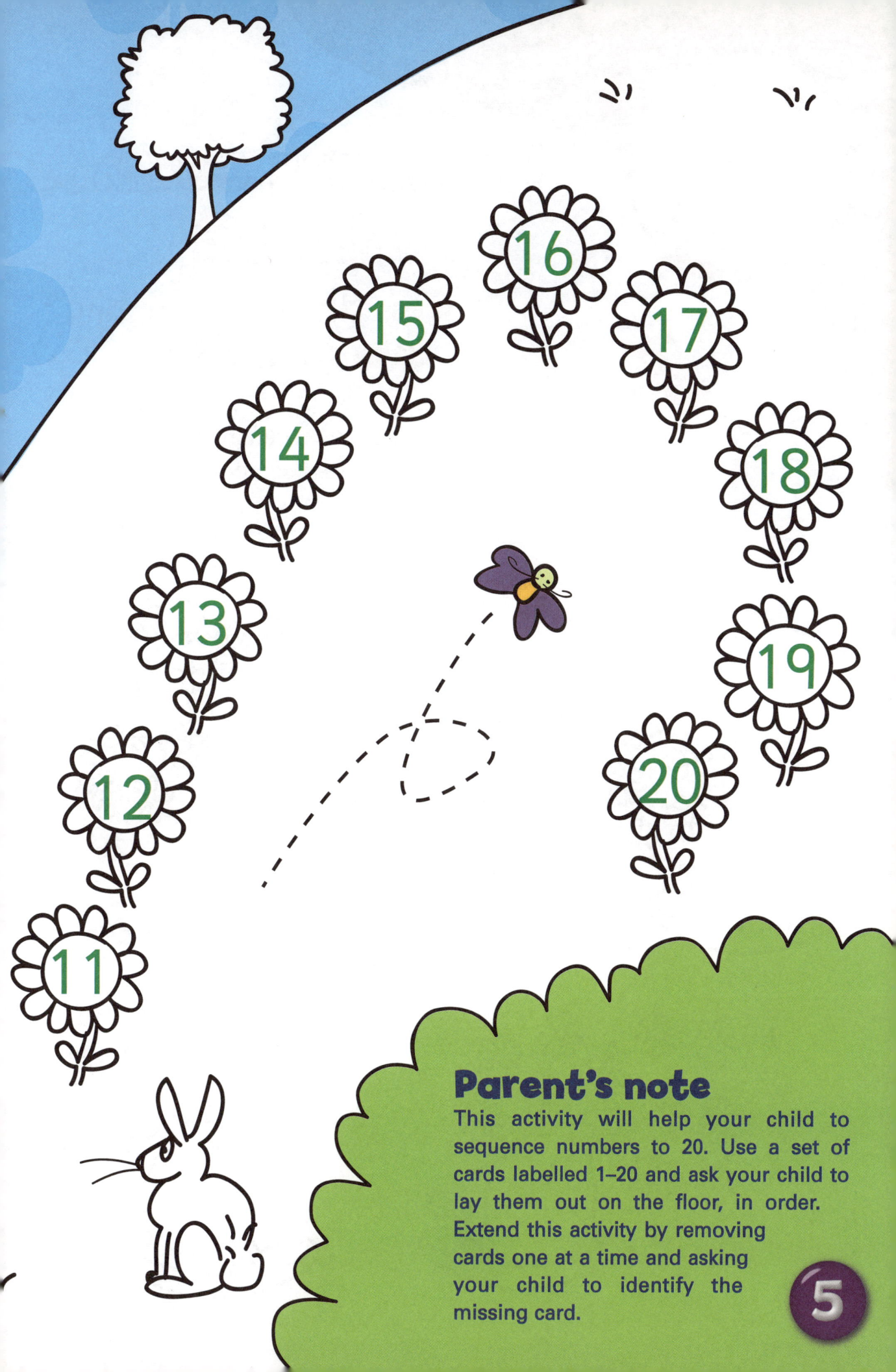

Parent's note

This activity will help your child to sequence numbers to 20. Use a set of cards labelled 1–20 and ask your child to lay them out on the floor, in order. Extend this activity by removing cards one at a time and asking your child to identify the missing card.

Princess counts to 20

Princess the pig is counting daisies in the field.

Help her to count the number of daisies in each group. Write the answer on the snail.

a

b

c

d

g

e

h

f

Parent's note
This activity will help your child to count reliably to 20. Make a habit of counting during everyday activities, such as peeling potatoes, going upstairs, etc.

7

Horace has sugar lumps

Horace the horse loves sugar lumps!

Count the sugar lumps in each group.
Join the group to the correct number with a line.

19

16

10

14

a

b

c

d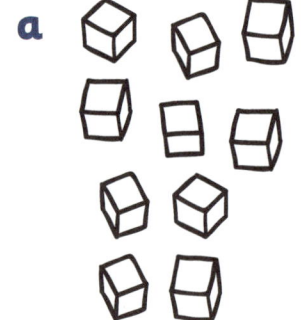

e

12

11

15

18

f

g

h

Parent's note

This activity gives your child practice with counting up to 20. Make a collection of found objects, such as shells, acorns, etc. to use for counting activities. Tell your child to bring you a bag filled with 15 acorns, 12 grapes, etc.

Daffodil counts creatures

Daffodil the dog gets very excited when she sees all the wildlife that lives on the farm.

Count the creatures with her, then write the number in the big flower.

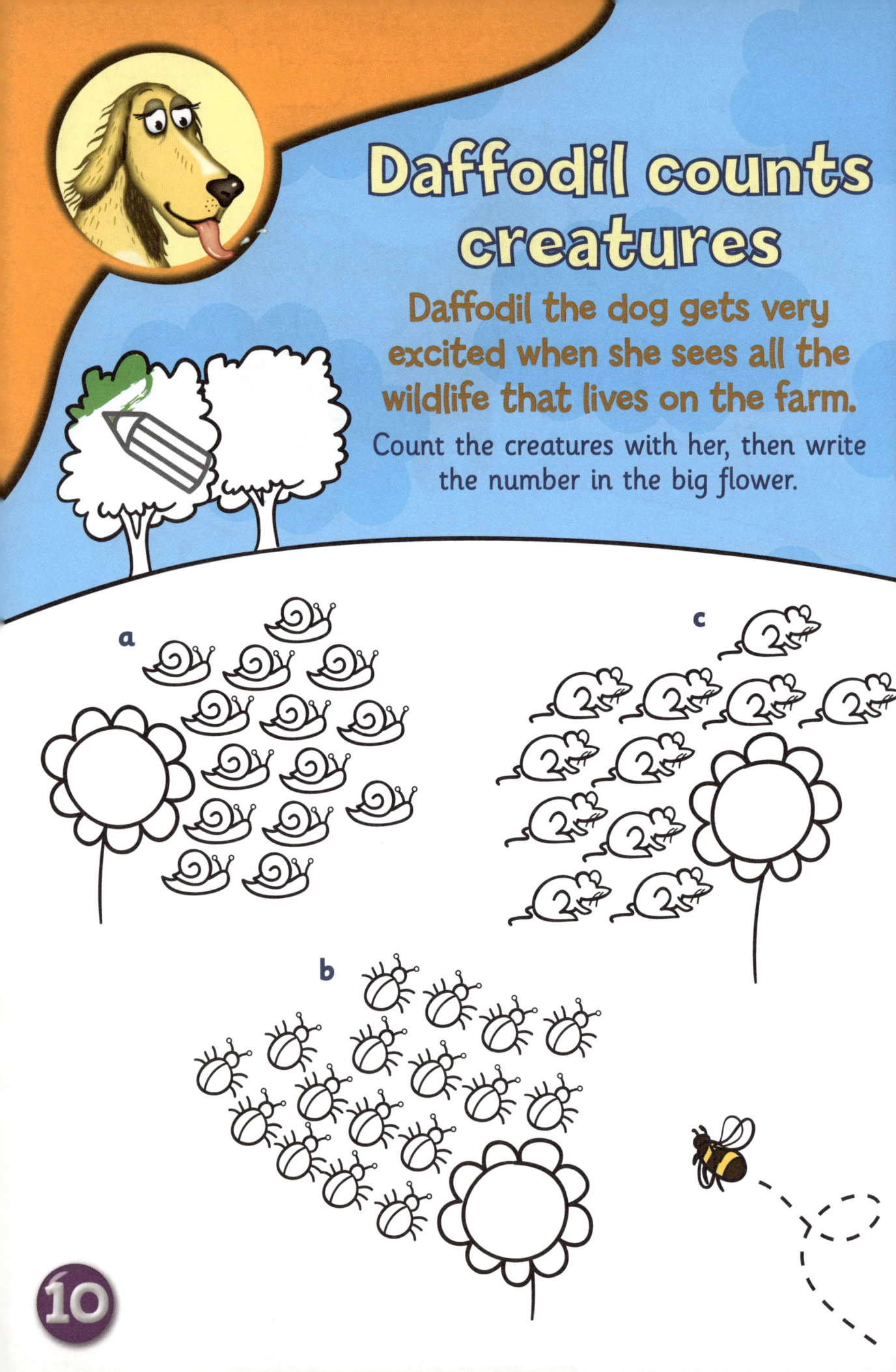

a

b

c

d

f

g

e

Parent's note
Your child will need lots of practice counting up to 20 – many children find the 'teens' numbers difficult. Encourage your child to count toys as she puts them away, or biscuits as they are put on a plate.

Fun time!

Join the dots to see which Fun Farmyard friend is standing by the barn.

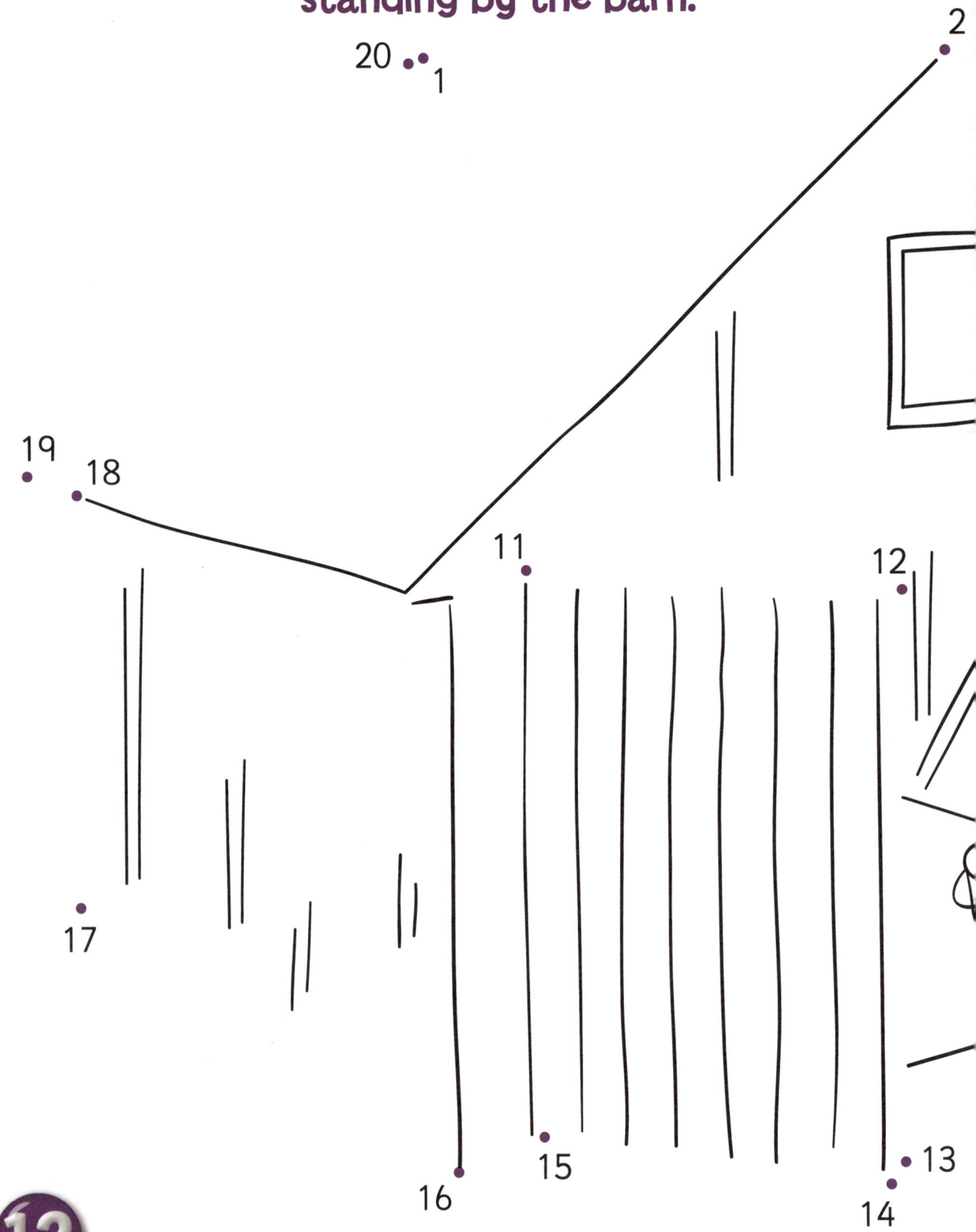

20 1

2

19

18

11

12

17

16 15

13

14

Parent's note

Dot-to-dot exercises are fun to do and teach your child about sequencing numbers. Encourage your child to say the numbers as he joins them, to help embed the sequence in his memory.

13

Sebastian dreams of numbers

Sebastian the sheep is daydreaming. He is looking at the shape of the clouds.

Some of these clouds look like numbers. Write the number on the clouds.

10 · 16 · 19

Parent's note

This activity encourages your child to learn the shapes of the numerals to 20. Give him physical experiences of tracing numbers in sand, salt, flour, etc. so he gets a physical memory of the shape of the numbers.

15

Candy counts in 2s

Candy the cat has two bells on her collar.

Look at the pictures of her bells. Use the number line to help you count in 2s. Write the number of bells on the cat shape.

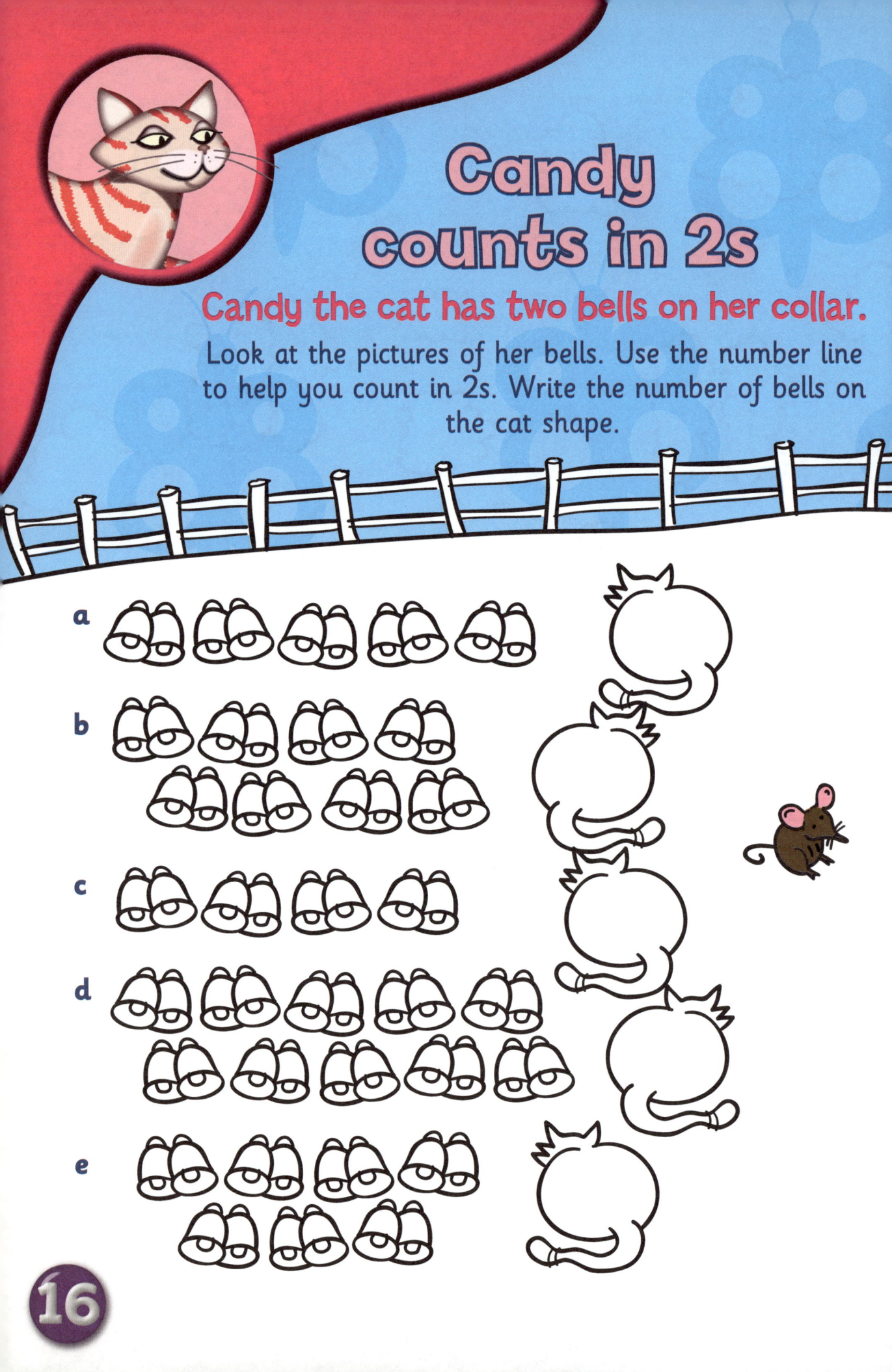

a

b

c

d

e

f

g

h

17

Henrietta counts in 10s

Henrietta the hen and her chicks love to eat seeds. Each sack holds 10 kilogrammes.

Count in 10s, using the number line to help you. Write the total number on the egg.

10 20 30 40 50 60 70 80 90 100

a

10 10 10

c

10 10 10 10 10 10
10 10 10 10

b

10 10 10 10
10 10 10
10 10 10

d

10 10 10
10

18

19

Terence looks at numbers

Terence the tractor has a number on his back. It is written with a number – and a number word!

Write the numbers on each tractor shape.

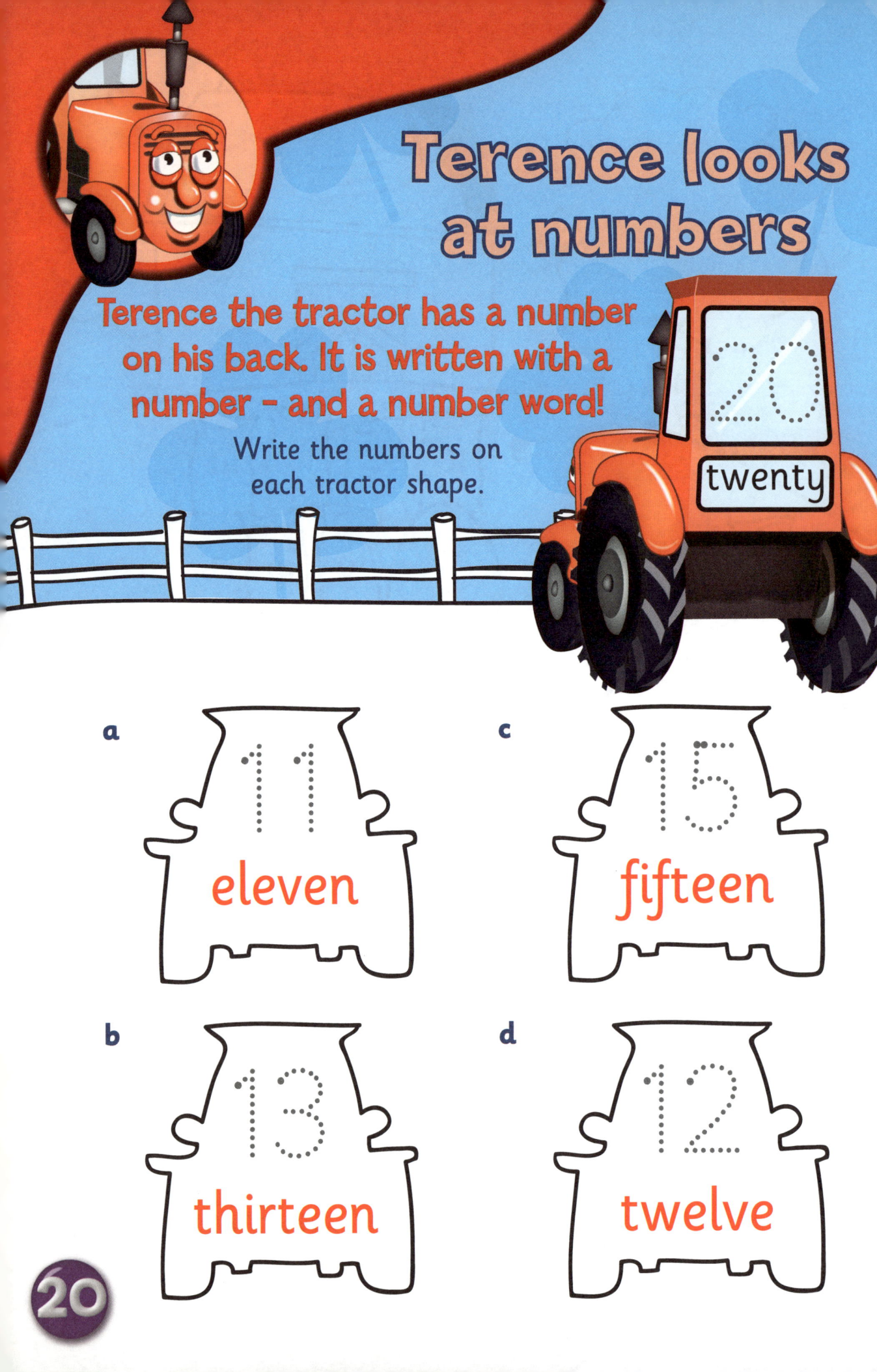

20

twenty

a 11 eleven

b 13 thirteen

c 15 fifteen

d 12 twelve

e **16**

sixteen

g **17**

seventeen

f **19**

nineteen

Princess gets muddy

Princess the pig is jumping in mud puddles in the field.

Fill in the missing numbers. They have been covered in mud!

a 0 1 2 3 4 ⬚ 6 7 ⬚ 9 ⬚
⬚ 12 ⬚ 14 ⬚ 16 17 ⬚ 19 20

b 0 1 2 3 4 5 6 7 8 9 ⬚
⬚ ⬚ 13 ⬚ ⬚ 16 17 18 19 ⬚

c ⬚ 1 ⬚ 3 4 5 6 7 8 9 10
11 12 ⬚ ⬚ 15 ⬚ 17 18 ⬚ 20

d 0 1 2 3 4 5 6 7 8 9 10
11 ⬚ 13 ⬚ 15 ⬚ 17 ⬚ 19 ⬚

22

e 0 1 2 3 4 5 6 7 8 9 10
12 14 16 17 20

f 0 1 2 3 4 5 6 7 8 9 10
11 13 14 18

Parent's note

This activity will help your child to become familiar with the number sequence from 0–20. Make a number line of cards 0–20 on a washing line. Write the number on the card as a numeral and a word. Hold the cards on the line with pegs or tape.

23

Fun time!

Here are the Fun Farmyard friends,
playing in the vegetable garden.
Why don't you colour them in?

Parent's note

Colouring in is not just a time filler. It supports the development of fine motor skills in your child's hands and fingers. These skills will help her to hold pencils and crayons, and this will benefit her writing and drawing skills.

25

Horace looks and learns

Horace the horse is looking at the numbers on the stable doors.

Look at the numbers on the doors, then copy them onto the top half of the stable doors.

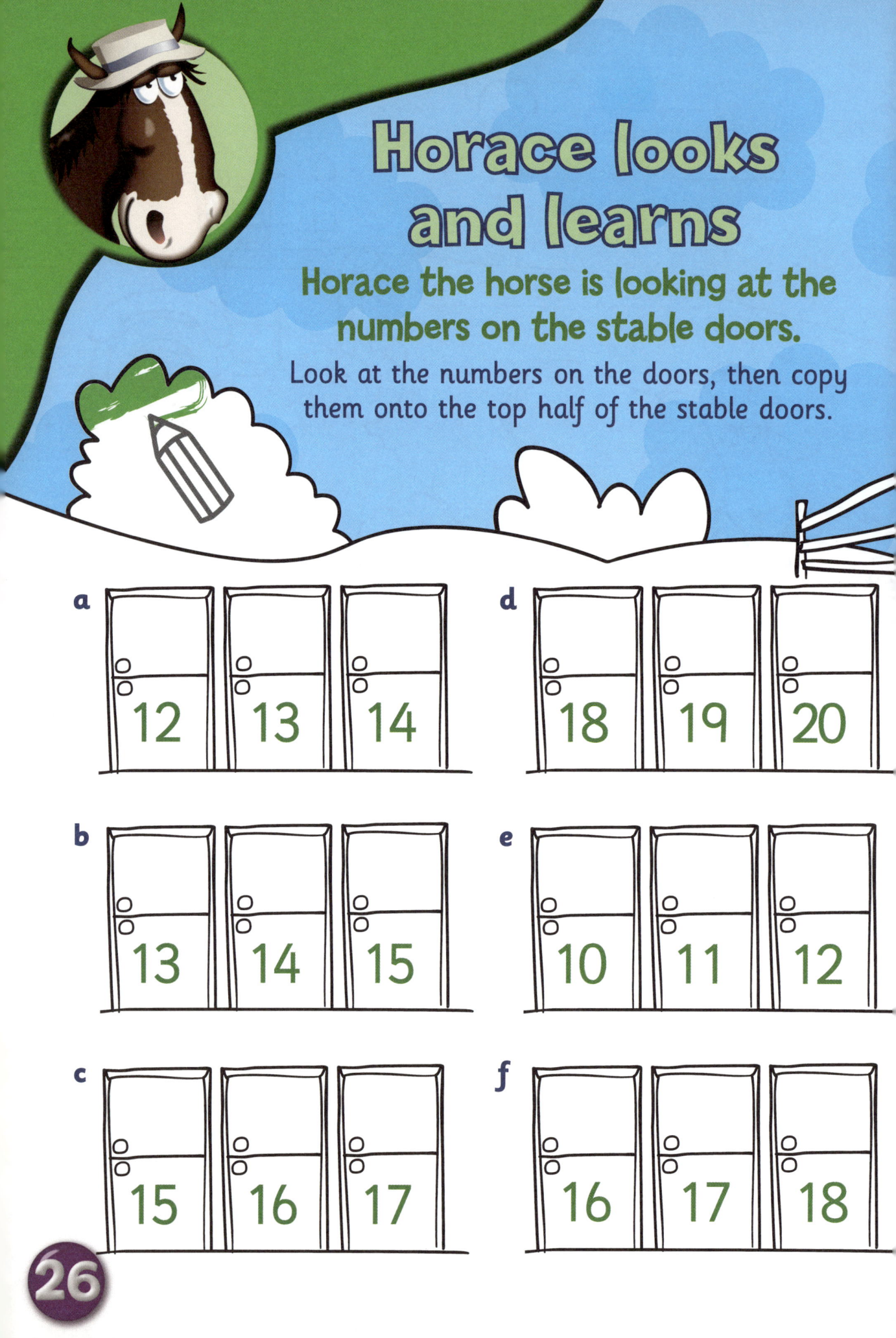

a
12 13 14

d
18 19 20

b
13 14 15

e
10 11 12

c
15 16 17

f
16 17 18

26

g

11	12	13

h

14	15	16

20

Parent's note
This activity will help your child to sequence numbers between 0 and 20. Count to 20 with your child, taking turns to say alternate numbers.

27

Terence counts sacks

Terence the tractor is bringing sacks of corn back to the barn on his trailer.

Count the sacks in each trailer.
Write the number on the side of the tractor.

a

b

c

d

e

f

Parent's note
This activity will reinforce your child's ability to count to 20. Encourage your child to count wherever you are – stones on the beach, trees in the woods, etc. until it becomes second nature.

29

Candy's cosy bed

Candy the cat likes to sleep in a cosy bed.

In each pair, colour the bed with the **most** pillows pink and the **least** pillows blue.

a

b

c

d

e

f

Parent's note

This activity teaches your child about the concepts of 'more' and 'less'. Use practical experiences to develop the idea, such as putting cakes or biscuits on plates and asking your child which plate has more/less.

31

Gus gets hungry

Gus the goat has been very naughty. He has been chewing washing off the line!

1 2 3 4 5 6 7 8 9 10 11 12 13 14 15 16 17 18 19 20

Write the missing **odd** numbers in the boxes.
Use the sock number line to help you.

a 10 ☐ 12 ☐ 14 ☐ 16

b 14 ☐ 16 ☐ 18 ☐ 20

c 6 ☐ 8 ☐ 10 ☐ 12

Now write the missing even numbers in these boxes.

d 9 ☐ 11 ☐ 13 ☐ 15

e 11 ☐ 13 ☐ 15 ☐ 17

f 13 ☐ 15 ☐ 17 ☐ 19

Parent's note

This activity will familiarise your child with odd and even numbers. Help your child by making a number line from 1–20. Cut out pieces of scrap card and write the odd numbers in red and the even numbers in blue. Look at the numbers together, explaining that even numbers are those that can be shared between two with nothing left over. Demonstrate by sharing 2, 4, 6 grapes, peanuts, etc. with your child.

Fun time!

Here is a creature that lives on the flowers in the field. Colour all the numbers that end in zero red. Colour all the odd numbers black. What can you see?

12

14

16

2

4

18

20

10

6

15

8

20

13

12

17

14

10

11

18

9

12

4

Henrietta crunches corn

Henrietta the hen is eating some nice, crunchy corn.

Each pile of corn started with 20. How many has Henrietta eaten from each pile? Write the answer on the sack.

a

b

c

d

36

e

g

h

f

Parent's note

This activity will encourage your child to use 'counting on' to find the difference between two numbers. Help your child to understand by making groups of small toys such as toy cars, bricks, etc. and asking him to count on to make 20.

37

Clover collects leaves

Clover the cow is collecting clover leaves.

Find the pairs of clover leaves that add together to make 20 and join them with a line.

Parent's note

This activity introduces your child to the number bonds (pairs of numbers) that make a total of 20. Make a card game by writing the numbers 0–20 on 21 pieces of card. Write the corresponding number to make 20 on the back of each card, such as 0 and 20, 1 and 19, 2 and 18, etc. Use them as flashcards and encourage your child to guess the number on the back of each card.

Sebastian counts birds

Sebastian the sheep likes watching swallows flying in the sky.

Count the birds in each set. Write the answer in the cloud.

Parent's note

This activity gives your child more practice with counting to 20. Encourage your child to make a number poster for her bedroom wall. On a large piece of paper, draw a grid so there are 20 squares. Get her to write the numbers 1–20, one number in the corner of each square. Then she can draw the correct number of pictures in each square (1 cat, 2 ducks, 3 rabbits – whatever she chooses).

41

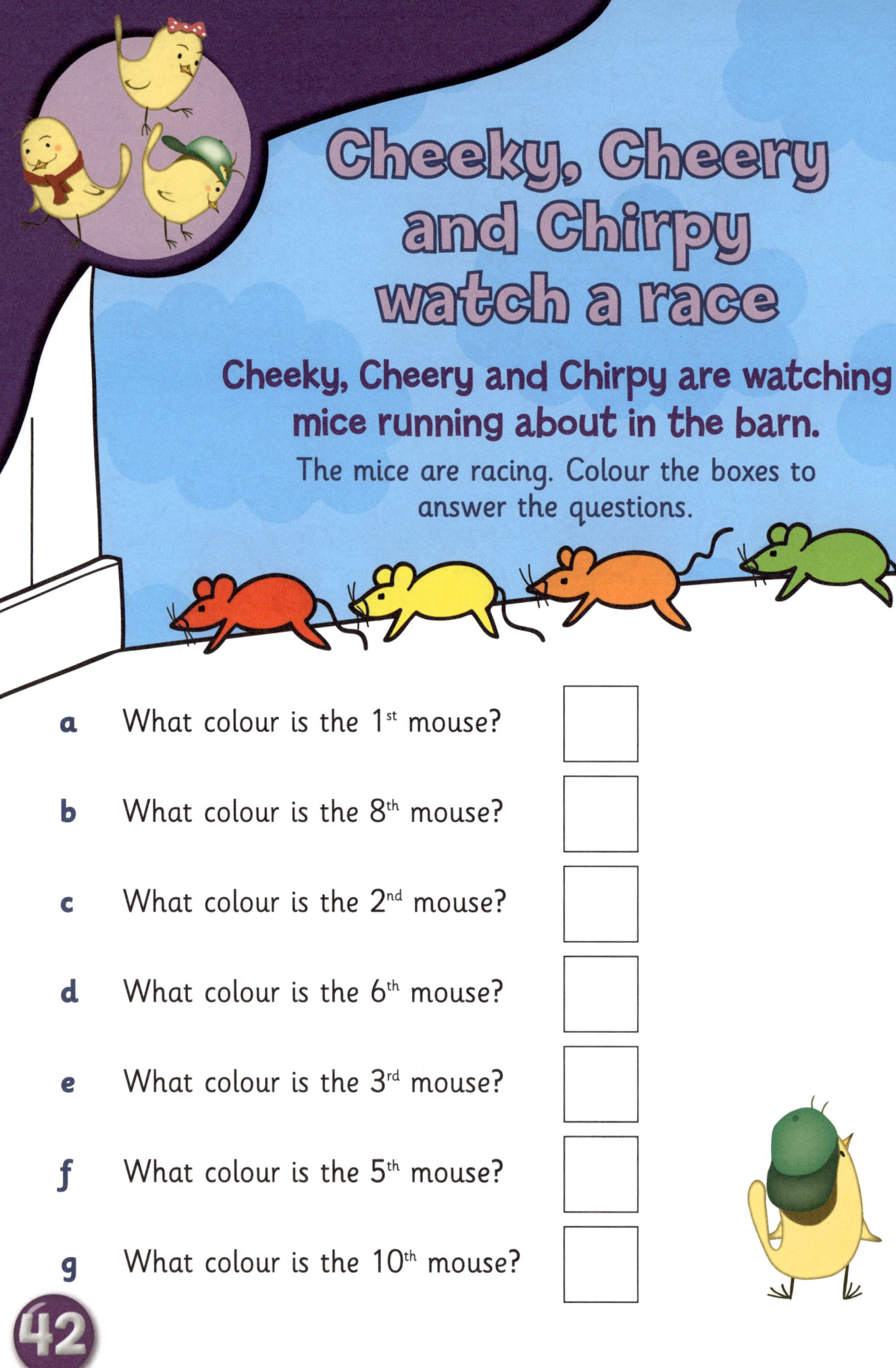

Cheeky, Cheery and Chirpy watch a race

Cheeky, Cheery and Chirpy are watching mice running about in the barn.

The mice are racing. Colour the boxes to answer the questions.

a What colour is the 1st mouse?

b What colour is the 8th mouse?

c What colour is the 2nd mouse?

d What colour is the 6th mouse?

e What colour is the 3rd mouse?

f What colour is the 5th mouse?

g What colour is the 10th mouse?

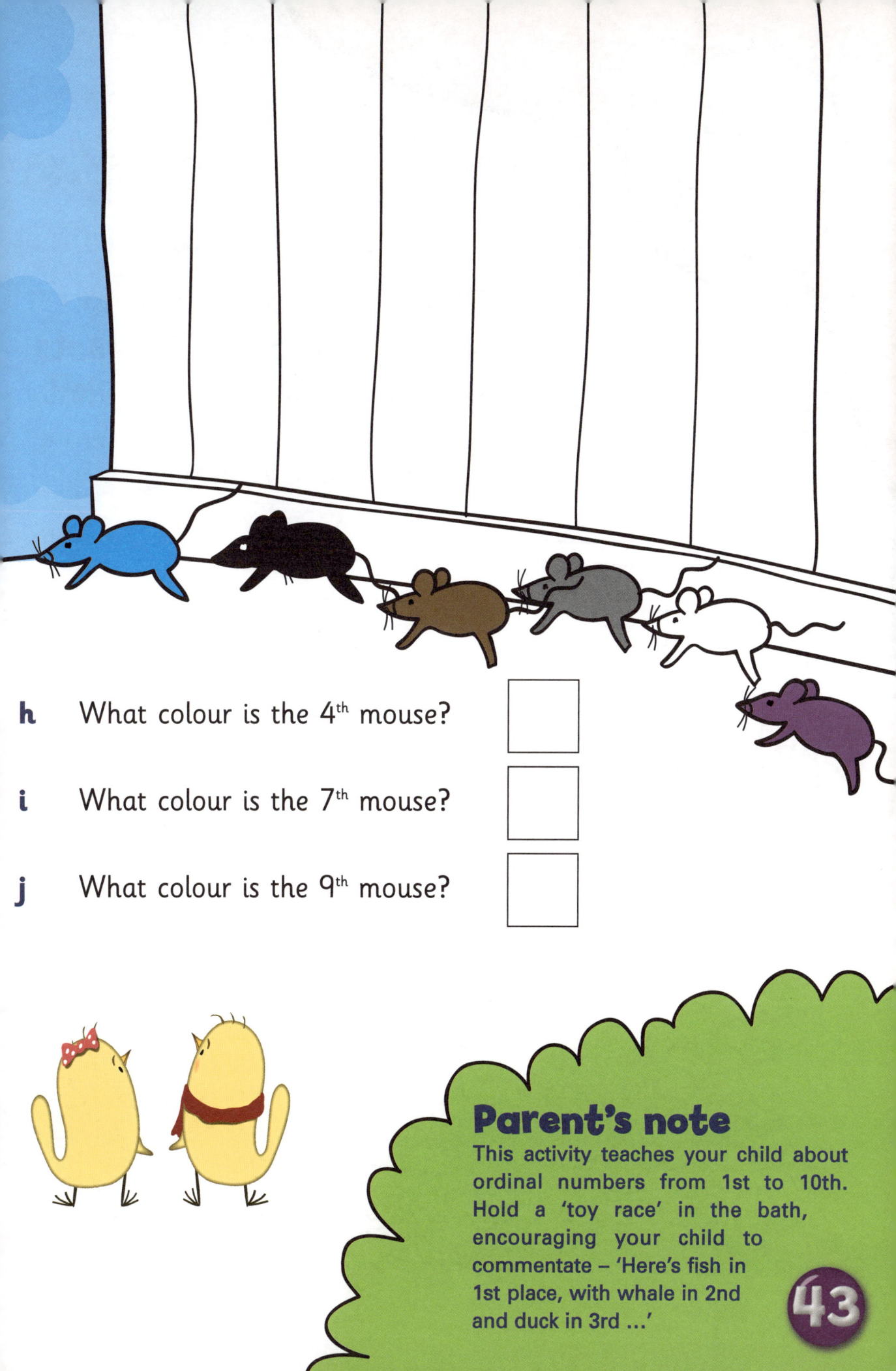

h What colour is the 4th mouse?

i What colour is the 7th mouse?

j What colour is the 9th mouse?

Parent's note

This activity teaches your child about ordinal numbers from 1st to 10th. Hold a 'toy race' in the bath, encouraging your child to commentate – 'Here's fish in 1st place, with whale in 2nd and duck in 3rd ...'

43

Daffodil counts biscuits

Daffodil the dog is eating yummy dog biscuits. She wants to know how many she has left.

Count the biscuits in each group. Write the number on the bag.

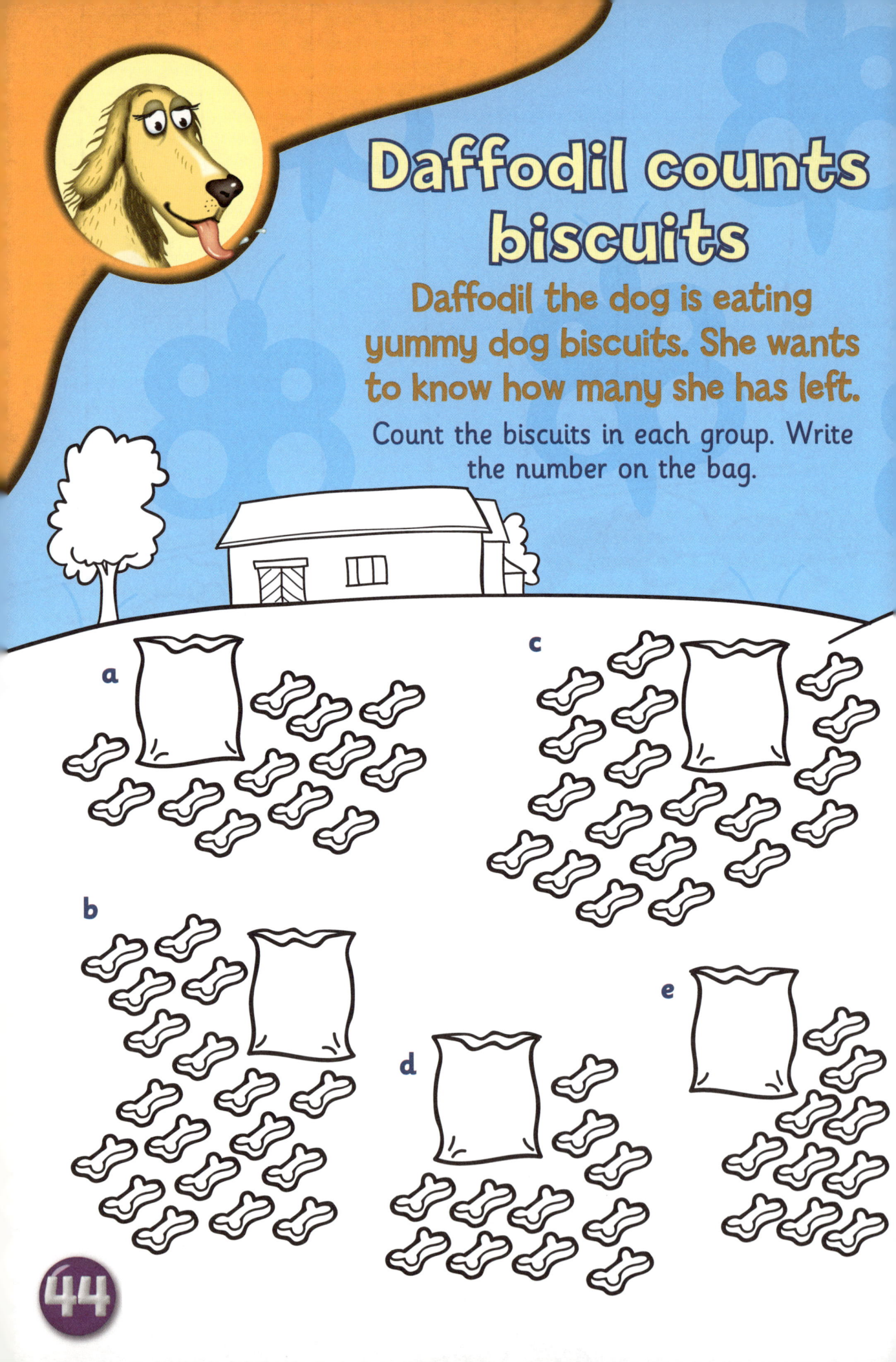

a

b

c

d

e

f

g

h

Parent's note

This activity gives your child more practice with counting to 20. Encourage your child to count in practical situations, such as doing up buttons, eating pumpkin seeds, putting things away, etc.

45

Answers

Pages 4–5
Ensure child says each number correctly before colouring in the appropriate flower.

Pages 6–7
a	15	e	14
b	12	f	11
c	18	g	13
d	19	h	20

Pages 8–9

Pages 10–11
a	14	e	12
b	17	f	19
c	11	g	13
d	15		

Pages 12–13
Dots joined to reveal Clover the cow standing by the barn.

Pages 14–15

Pages 16–17
a	10	e	14
b	16	f	12
c	8	g	18
d	20	h	6

Pages 18–19
a	30	e	50
b	80	f	70
c	100	g	60
d	40	h	90

Pages 20–21
a	11	e	16
b	13	f	19
c	15	g	17
d	12		

Pages 22–23
a	5, 8, 10, 11, 13, 15, 18
b	10, 11, 12, 14, 15, 20
c	0, 2, 13, 14, 16, 19
d	12, 14, 16, 18, 20
e	11, 13, 15, 18, 19
f	12, 15, 16, 17, 19, 20

Pages 24–25
Picture coloured in as neatly as possible.

Pages 26–27
a	12, 13, 14	e	10, 11, 12
b	13, 14, 15	f	16, 17, 18
c	15, 16, 17	g	11, 12, 13
d	18, 19, 20	h	14, 15, 16

Pages 28–29

a	11	**d**	13
b	14	**e**	10
c	12	**f**	16

Pages 30–31

Pages 32–33

a 11, 13, 15
b 15, 17, 19
c 7, 9, 11
d 10, 12, 14
e 12, 14, 16
f 14, 16, 18

Pages 34–35

Picture of a ladybird revealed by colouring in sections.

Pages 36–37

a	7	**e**	5
b	6	**f**	8
c	4	**g**	2
d	1	**h**	3

Pages 38–39

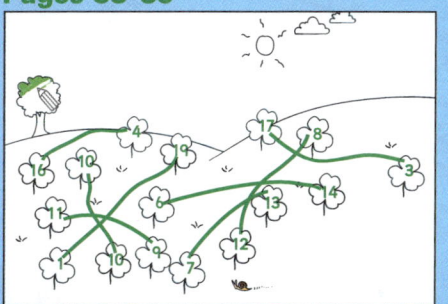

Pages 40–41

a	19	**e**	17
b	10	**f**	15
c	18	**g**	11
d	12	**h**	14

Pages 42–43

a red
b grey
c yellow
d black
e orange
f blue
g purple
h green
i brown
j white

Pages 44–45

a	12	**e**	10
b	18	**f**	20
c	19	**g**	13
d	11	**h**	17

Goodbye!

Just colour us in before you go.